Morals and Markets

Seventh Annual IEA Hayek Memorial Lecture

Given in London on Tuesday, 2 June 1998

Professor Jonathan Sacks
Chief Rabbi of the United Hebrew Congregations of the Commonwealth

With commentaries by

Professor Norman Barry
Professor Robert Davidson
Professor Michael Novak

Published by The Institute of Economic Affairs
1999
Second Impression 2000

First published in May 1999
Second Impression May 2000
by
The Institute of Economic Affairs
2 Lord North Street
Westminster
London SW1P 3LB

Occasional Paper 108
ISSN 0073-909X
ISBN 0-255 36424-5

Many IEA publications are translated into languages other than English
or are reprinted. Permission to translate or to reprint should be sought
from the General Director at the address above.

Printed in Great Britain by
Hartington Fine Arts Limited, Lancing, West Sussex
Set in Times New Roman 11 on 13 point

Contents

Foreword

IT MAY BE TRUE THAT 'EVERYONE BELIEVES IN MARKETS NOW' but there are many opinions on the place of morality in market systems and on the origins of moral views.

The thoughts of such an eminent author in this field as Professor Jonathan Sacks are of great interest, and so the Institute was particularly pleased when he agreed to give the 1998 IEA Hayek Memorial Lecture. The Lecture was so memorable an experience for those present that it seemed appropriate to ask other distinguished people to express their thoughts on Professor Sacks' views, in the form of commentaries on his paper.

This Occasional Paper reproduces Professor Sacks' Lecture, as presented, together with commentaries by Professors Norman Barry, Robert Davidson and Michael Novak. There is then an Afterword by Professor Sacks.

As in all IEA publications, the views expressed are those of the authors, not those of the Institute (which has no corporate view), its Trustees, Advisers or Directors. But the Institute commends Occasional Paper 108 to its readers for its stimulating ideas on how morals and markets are related.

March 1999   COLIN ROBINSON
Editorial Director, Institute of Economic Affairs,
Professor of Economics, University of Surrey

The Authors

RABBI PROFESSOR JONATHAN SACKS has been Chief Rabbi of the United Hebrew Congregations of the Commonwealth since 1 September 1991, the sixth incumbent since 1845.

At the time his appointment was announced, he was Principal of Jews' College, London, the world's oldest rabbinical seminary, where he also held the Chair in Modern Jewish Thought and instituted novel programmes in rabbinic pre- and in-service training. He himself gained his rabbinic ordination from Jews' College as well as from London's Yeshiva Etz Chaim. He has been rabbi of the Golders Green and Marble Arch Synagogues in London.

He was educated at Gonville and Caius College, Cambridge, where he obtained first class honours in Philosophy, and pursued postgraduate studies at New College, Oxford, and King's College, London. In 1990 he delivered the BBC Reith Lectures on *The Persistence of Faith.*

Professor Sacks has been Visiting Professor of Philosophy at the University of Essex, Sherman Lecturer at Manchester University, Riddell Lecturer at Newcastle University, and Cook Lecturer at the Universities of Oxford, Edinburgh and St Andrews. In 1997, he delivered the first Yerusha [Jewish Heritage] Lecture at Cambridge University. He holds honorary doctorates from the universities of Cambridge, Middlesex, Haifa, Yeshiva University, New York, Liverpool and St Andrews, and is an honorary fellow of Gonville and Caius College, Cambridge, and King's College, London. He is currently Visiting Professor of Theology and Religious Studies, and during 1998 became Visiting Professor of the Hebrew University, Jerusalem. In 1995, he received the Jerusalem Prize for his contribution to diaspora Jewish life.

The Chief Rabbi is a frequent contributor to radio, television and the national press. He is the author of 11 books, including *Tradition in an Untraditional Age* (1990), *The Persistence of Faith* (1991), *Arguments for the Sake of Heaven* (1991), *Crisis and*

Covenant (1992), *One People?* (1993), *Will We Have Jewish Grandchildren?* (1994), *Community of Faith* (1995), and *The Politics of Hope* (1997).

NORMAN BARRY is Professor of Social and Political Theory at the University of Buckingham. He has previously taught at the Queen's University, Belfast, and the University of Central England. He was Visiting Scholar at the Social Philosophy and Policy Center, Bowling Green State University, Ohio, 1989-90, and at Liberty Fund, Indianapolis, 1994-95. He specialises in political theory, welfare theory and business ethics. His books include *Hayek's Social and Economic Philosophy* (1979), *An Introduction to Modern Political Theory* (3rd edition, 1995), and *Business Ethics* (1998). He has contributed widely to academic journals. He is a member of the Academic Advisory Councils of the Institute of Economic Affairs (London) and the David Hume Institute (Edinburgh).

THE VERY REVD PROFESSOR ROBERT DAVIDSON, MA, BD, DD, FRSE, was born in Markinch, Fife, in 1927. He graduated in Classics and Divinity, Old Testament Studies, from the University of St Andrews and then lectured in the Universities of Aberdeen, St Andrews and Edinburgh before taking up appointment as Professor of Old Testament Language and Literature in the University of Glasgow in 1972. He retired in 1991. In 1989, he delivered the Edward Cadbury Lectures in the University of Birmingham and he has also lectured in the USA, Canada and Malawi. He was elected Moderator of the General Assembly of the Church of Scotland in 1990. He has published extensively in the field of Old Testament Studies, the most recent being *The Vitality of Worship* (Eerdmans, Hansel Press, 1998), a commentary on the Psalms. He is married with eight children, four of whom are adopted.

MICHAEL NOVAK is the Director of Social and Political Studies at the American Enterprise Institute in Washington, DC, where he also holds the George Frederick Jewett Chair in Religion and Public Policy. His best known book is *The Spirit of Democratic Capitalism* (1982), which was widely influential in Poland,

Czechoslovakia, and later America during the 1980s. *The New Consensus on Family and Welfare* (1987), a seminar report of which he was the principal author, is considered a watershed study in welfare reform in the US, and in this connection he has been a frequent lecturer at the Institute of Economic Affairs in London. For the originality of his work in theology and economics, he was awarded the Templeton Prize for Progress in Religion, at Buckingham Palace in 1994. For the IEA he has written *Morality, Capitalism and Democracy* (1990); *Awakening from Nihilism* (1995); and *Is There a Third Way?* (1998).

Morals and Markets
Professor Jonathan Sacks

IN 1978, FRIEDRICH HAYEK, WHOSE WORK AND INFLUENCE we commemorate tonight, proposed a great debate. He was by then almost 80 years old, but the passion with which he sought to defend the market order against what he saw as the heresy of collectivism was undiminished. So, as if hoping to settle the issue once and for all, he suggested nothing less than an international disputation that would discuss the question, 'Was socialism a mistake?' The event did not take place, but Hayek none the less produced a large manuscript setting out his beliefs, which was published in an abridged form under the title, *The Fatal Conceit*.[1] What interests me in particular about this work is the title of the book's last chapter, namely, 'Religion and the Guardians of Tradition'. What led Hayek, who had devoted a lifetime to the study of economics and politics, to set the seal on this work with a reflection on religion and tradition?

The Fatal Conceit is a difficult book, but if I have understood it correctly, its argument is this. For the free market and its 'extended order' to emerge, so too did a certain kind of morality. For many thousands of years, human beings had lived in small bands of hunter-gatherers, and it was during that long pre-history of *homo sapiens* that our instincts were formed. Those instincts – of solidarity and altruism – allowed our ancestors to live together in close face-to-face groups and without them no isolated individual could have survived for very long.

However, a significant change had to take place in the way people related to one another for mankind to be able to make the transition from the small group or tribe to the larger and more open associations needed for complex societies and economies. Instincts were no longer sufficient. Instead their place had to be taken by rules such as those relating to private property, honesty, contract, exchange and so on. For Hayek, the question of how these rules

---

[1] F. A. Hayek, *The Fatal Conceit: The Errors of Socialism*, London: Routledge, 1988.

first appeared is irrelevant. What matters is that they emerged and spread, not because people were able to decide in advance what their consequences would be, but simply because the groups who adhered to them found themselves able to grow and spread more successfully than others.

Often they involved people acting against their instincts, so they had to be taught through habit rather than by appeal to inclination. Moral education became a matter of imitation, learning by doing, the handing on of tradition by habituation. Morality itself consisted largely of 'Thou shalt not's', prohibitions that served as boundaries within which free human action could be directed and contained, much as the banks of a river contain and direct the flow of water. It was this kind of morality that, for Hayek, made possible the fateful transition of humanity from tribal society to a market economy in which ever larger associations of individuals and groups could develop their specialisations and yet meet their needs through the peaceful process of trade and exchange.

So it was in the past. But Hayek, having lived through some of the great dislocations of the 20th century, could never take the market order or its associated phenomenon, the free society, for granted. It was, he believed, vulnerable on two counts. On the one hand there was the perennial danger of a retreat into the primitive instinct of group solidarity with its attendant hatred of the outsider. On the other there was the seductive voice of reason, the 'fatal conceit' that by conscious intent and deliberate planning we can improve on the morality of the past, and as it were re-design our basic human institutions. This, he felt, was the error of socialism, but not only socialism. It was also the mistake of liberals such as John Stuart Mill who regarded traditional moral constraints as, for the most part, eminently dispensable, the unwanted baggage of a more superstitious age. Morality – as Hayek never tires of reminding us in the course of the book – occupies a place *between* instinct and reason and cannot be reduced to either.

This line of thought brought Hayek to reflect on the role of religion – in particular the great monotheistic faiths – in preserving moral traditions. In part this was a matter of history. We owe it to religions, he said:

> 'that beneficial traditions have been preserved and transmitted at least long enough to enable those groups following them to grow, and to

have the opportunity to spread by natural or cultural selection.'[2]

But it was not only a matter of history; it was a matter of the present as well. To understand why, we have to remind ourselves again of Hayek's understanding of the 'extended order' of complex societies. They come about, he argues, because of repeated applications of simple rules. They develop in ways which none of us can predict in advance. Each one of us plays a minute but significant part in that process. We participate, in his powerful phrase, in 'those spontaneous social forces through which the individual creates things greater than he knows'. Only with hindsight and historical perspective can we see what, through an almost infinite number of individual acts, we have achieved. None of us, not the wisest of sages or the most informed of central agencies, could have planned it in advance.

The striking feature of religion, for Hayek, is its attitude of humility, even reverence, towards the great moral institutions without which our 'extended order' could not have developed. It guards against what he calls 'the rationalist delusion that man, by exercising his intelligence, invented morals that gave him the power to achieve more than he could ever foresee'. Of course it does so by insisting that our morals were given by God. For Hayek, they were arrived at by the evolutionary forces of history. What these two views held in common, though, was a strong and principled opposition to the idea that individually or collectively we can devise a better system rationally constructed to maximise happiness or some other good.

It is a fascinating argument, and it places Hayek in a line of thinkers – such as Edmund Burke, Max Weber, and most recently Francis Fukuyama – who have reflected not only on the internal morality of markets (what we call nowadays 'business ethics') but on the wider question of what kind of society gives rise to and is able to sustain a market economy. The answer which each of them gave – an answer that has been given new salience by the rise of the economies of South East Asia – is that they tend to be societies with a strong respect for certain kinds of tradition.

Like Burke, Hayek combines liberalism in economics and

---

[2]   F. A. Hayek, *ibid.*, p. 136.

politics with a marked conservatism in morality. Free institutions, they seem to say, are best preserved by a certain piety towards the past. Traditions encode the accumulated discoveries of earlier generations in a way that no single generation, however sophisticated, could discover for itself; and it is through learning those traditions and passing them on to our children that we avoid extremely costly mistakes. Paradoxically, it may be just those societies that have strong religious and moral habits, which form the best environment for economic development and technological innovation. It may be that those who are most secure in their past are the most confident and energetic in shaping the future.

Thus far Hayek; and it is an argument that is worth revisiting, for the very opposite reason than the one he contemplated. *The Fatal Conceit* was written in 1978 and published in 1988. Twenty years ago, he could still see socialism as the dragon to be slain. Within a year, though, of the book's publication, the Berlin Wall came down. In rapid succession, the Cold War ended, East European communism was abandoned, and the Soviet Union was disbanded. It was one of the most decisive victories in the history of ideologies, all the more striking for having taken place without a shot being fired. Hayek's great debate never took place, but it is fair to say, as of now, that he won the argument after all. As Raymond Plant put it: 'Central economic planning is now not on the political agenda of any country seeking to be part of the global economy.'[3]

It is therefore all the more important for us to bear in mind the caveat Hayek himself insisted on, namely that the market economy can only be sustained by certain habits of behaviour and restraint which he called traditions. He believed that the threat to these traditions was socialism. Doubtless, in his day it was. But what he paid far less attention to was the possibility that they might be undermined not by anti-market ideologies but by the very power of the market itself. For the market is not only an institution of exchange. It is also a highly anti-traditional force, at least in advanced consumer societies. The stimulation of demand, for example, depends on a culture, even a cult, of the new, the product

---

[3] Lord Plant, *Markets, Morals and Community*, Twentieth Annual Lecture, St. George's House, Windsor, 1997, p. 3.

that improves on the past and renders it obsolete in an increasingly short space of time. It encourages a view of human life itself as a series of consumer choices rather than as a set of inherited ways of doing things.

One of the most fateful developments is the displacement of human identity as something given by the history into which I am born. Instead it becomes something like a suit of clothes which I can choose, wear for a while, and then discard in favour of the new season's fashion – the move graphically illustrated by our change of terminology from 'life' to 'life-style', with its suggestion that there is nothing of substance that defines who I am; there is merely the supermarket of ideas from which I can choose what I happen to be into for the time being, from Buddhism to therapy to aerobics to the environment to organic vegetables to the Internet to 'The Little Book of Calm'. In the process, religion itself is transformed from salvation to a branch of the leisure industry, and we are transformed, as one writer put it, 'from pilgrim to tourist'.

That is why it is sometimes useful to do what Hayek advised us to do in *The Fatal Conceit*, namely, to reflect on the role of religion in sustaining a particular kind of moral order. That is what I want to do, taking the experience of Jews and Judaism as an example. It was of course Max Weber, in his famous work on *The Protestant Ethic and the Spirit of Capitalism*,[4] who made us familiar with the idea that religion – in particular Calvinism – was one of the great shaping forces of the modern economy. More recently Michael Novak has written powerfully about the same subject from a Catholic perspective. But few writers have doubted the contribution Jews made to the development of finance, business and industry, a contribution that can be traced far back into the Middle Ages and beyond.

I vividly recall a talk given by the master of my college, the late Joseph Needham, describing the role Jews had played in bringing the inventions of China to the West. Christopher Columbus in his great journey of 1492, the year in which Jews were expelled from Spain, made use of tables drawn up by one Jew, Abraham Zacuto, instruments made by another, Joseph Vecinho, and took a third, Luis de Torres, as his interpreter. At about the same time, one of

---

[4] Translated by Talcott Parsons, London: Unwin, 1985.

the great rabbis and bible commentators of the Middle Ages, Don Yitzhak Abrabanel, served as financial advisor to King Alfonso V of Portugal and Ferdinand and Isabella of Castile, and later made important contributions to the economic life of Naples and Venice. Wherever they were able to, Jews played a significant role in the development of trade and finance. Indeed, in 1844, in a notoriously anti-semitic tract, Karl Marx argued that Jews were the very embodiment of the capitalist system.

It would be quite wrong to identify a great religious tradition with any particular set of economic institutions. It was, after all, the biblical Joseph who instituted the first known example of centralised economic planning, using the seven years of plenty to prepare for the seven years of famine, and whose ability to forecast trade cycles is probably still the envy of economists. Jewish history contains some of the great experiments in socialist utopias, from the property-sharing communities of the Essenes in the Second Temple period to the modern Israeli kibbutz. But there is no doubt that, for the most part, Jews and Judaism itself found free competition and trade the system most congruent with their values.

What was it about Judaism that led to this elective affinity between it and the market economy? In his stimulating recent book, *The Wealth and Poverty of Nations*,[5] David Landes identifies a number of factors. First there was the biblical respect for property rights. This he sees as nothing less than a revolution against the ancient world and the power it gave rulers to regard the property of the tribe or the people as their own. By contrast, when Moses finds his leadership challenged by the Israelites during the Korach rebellion, he says about his relation to the people: 'I have not taken one ass from them nor have I wronged any one of them.'

For a ruler to abuse property rights is, for the Hebrew Bible, one of the great corruptions of power. Judaism is the religion of a people born in slavery and longing for redemption; and the great assault of slavery against human dignity is that it deprives me of the ownership of the wealth I create. At the heart of the Hebrew Bible is the God who seeks the free worship of free human beings, and two of the most powerful defences of freedom are private

---

[5] David Landes, *The Wealth and Poverty of Nations*, London: Little, Brown, 1998, pp. 29-59.

property and economic independence. The ideal society envisaged by the prophets is one in which each person is able to sit 'underneath his own vine and fig tree'. The prophet Samuel in his famous speech on the dangers of monarchy – which might almost be subtitled *The Road to Serfdom* – warns against the constant temptation of kings to expropriate persons and property for the public good. Government, he seems to argue, may be necessary, but the less of it there is, the better.

Beyond this, Landes identifies in the Judaeo-Christian tradition, an openness to invention and innovation. In part this has to do with the biblical respect for labour. God tells Noah, for example, that he will be saved from the flood, but it is Noah who has to build the ark. The high value Judaism sets on work can be traced throughout the biblical and rabbinic literature. If not itself a religious act, it comes close to being a condition of the religious life. 'Six days shall you labour and do all your work, but the seventh day is a Sabbath to the Lord your God' – meaning that we serve God through work as well as rest. By our labour we become, in the striking rabbinic phrase, 'partners with God in the work of creation'.

The Jewish liturgy for Saturday night – the point at which the day of rest ends – culminates in a hymn to the values of work: 'When you eat of the labour of your hands, you are happy and it shall be well with you.' On this, the rabbis commented, 'You are happy' refers to this life; 'It shall be well with you' refers to life in the world to come. Work, in other words, has spiritual value, because earning our food is part of the essential dignity of the human condition. Animals *find* sustenance; only mankind *creates* it. As the 13th-century commentator Rabbenu Bachya put it: 'The active participation of man in the creation of his own wealth is a sign of his spiritual greatness.'

As a result, Judaism never developed either an aristocratic or a cloistered ethic that was dismissive of the productive economy. The great rabbis were themselves labourers or businessmen or professionals. They knew that the Jewish community needed an economic as well as a spiritual base. Accordingly, the Talmud lists as one of the duties of a parent, to teach one's child a craft or trade through which he can earn a living. Maimonides rules that one who is wise 'first establishes himself in an occupation which supports him, afterwards he buys a home, and after that he marries'. More powerful still is his ruling that to provide someone with a job is higher than any other form of welfare benefit:

> 'The highest degree of charity, exceeded by none, is that of a person who assists a poor Jew by providing him with a gift or a loan or by accepting him into a business partnership or by helping him to find employment – in a word, by putting him where he can dispense with other people's aid. With reference to such help it is said, 'You shall strengthen him, be he a stranger or a settler, he shall live with you' (Leviticus 25:35), which means to strengthen him in such a manner that his falling into want is prevented.'

All other forms of charity leave the recipient dependent on charity. Work alone restores his self-respect and independence. 'Flay carcasses in the market-place,' said the third-century teacher Rav, 'and do not say: I am a priest and a great man and it is beneath my dignity.'

No less important than the value placed on work is Judaism's positive attitude to the creation of wealth. The world is God's creation; therefore it is good, and prosperity is a sign of God's blessing. Asceticism and self-denial have little place in Jewish spirituality. What is more, God has handed the world over to human stewardship. The story of man's creation begins with the command, 'Be fruitful and multiply, fill the earth and subdue it'. God, taught Rabbi Akiva in the second century, deliberately left the world unfinished so that it could be completed by the work of man. Industry is more than mere labour. It is the arena in which we transform the world and thus become, in the striking rabbinic phrase, 'partners with God in the work of creation'.

It was Max Weber who observed that one of the revolutions of biblical thought was to demythologise, or disenchant, nature. For the first time human beings could see the condition of the world not as something given, sacrosanct and wrapped in mystery, but as something that could be rationally understood and improved upon. This perspective, central to Judaism, even today makes rabbinical authorities surprisingly open to new medical technologies such as genetic engineering and cloning, and tends to make religious Jews among the most dedicated users of the Internet and multi-media for purposes of education.

Above all, from a Jewish perspective, economic growth has

religious significance because it allows us to alleviate poverty. Judaism's early sages had the sanest view of poverty I know, and they did so because most of them were poor men. They refused theologically to anaesthetise its pain. They would utterly have rejected Marx's description of religion as the opium of the people. Poverty is not, in Judaism as in some faiths, a blessed condition. It is, the rabbis said, 'a kind of death' and 'worse than fifty plagues'. They said:

> 'Nothing is harder to bear than poverty, because he who is crushed by poverty is like one to whom all the troubles of the world cling and upon whom all the curses of Deuteronomy have descended. If all other troubles were placed on one side and poverty on the other, poverty would outweigh them all.'

What concerned the sages was not so much the elimination of poverty through redistributive taxation. Instead, what they sought to create was a society in which the poor had access to help when they needed it, through charity to be sure, but also and especially through job creation. Hence with wealth came responsibility. *Richesse oblige*. Successful businessmen (and women) were expected to set an example of philanthropy and to take on positions of communal leadership. Conspicuous consumption was frowned upon, and periodically banned through local 'sumptuary laws'. Wealth was a Divine blessing, and therefore it carried with it an obligation to use it for the benefit of the community as a whole.

Not the least significant of Judaic contributions to the development of Western civilisation was its emphasis on, perhaps even invention of, linear time. Ancient cultures tended to think of time as cyclical, seasonal, a matter of eternal recurrences to an original and unchanging nature of things. The Hebrew prophets were the first to see time in a quite different way – as a journey towards a destination, a narrative with a beginning and middle, even if the end (the messianic society) is always beyond the horizon. It is ultimately to this revolution that we owe the very notion of progress as an historical category, the idea that things are not predestined always to remain what they were. Hope, even more than necessity, is the mother of invention.

And to this we must add one further idea. The great

philosophical advocates of the market, Bernard Mandeville, David Hume, and Adam Smith, were struck by a phenomenon that many considered to be scandalous and amoral. This was their discovery that the market produced benefits to all through a series of actions and transactions that were essentially selfish in their motivation. As Adam Smith put it bluntly: 'It is not from the benevolence of the butcher, the brewer, or the baker, that we expect our dinner, but from their regard to their own interest.'[6] Within the system of free trade, as Smith put it most famously, the individual 'intends only his own gain, and he is, in this, as in many other cases, led by an invisible hand to promote an end which was no part of his intention'.[7] This fact, that markets and their associated institutions tend to work on the basis not of altruism but of somewhat earthier motives, has always led to a high-minded disdain for everything suggested by the word 'commercial'.

Not so within Judaism. Long before Mandeville and Adam Smith, Judaism had accepted the proposition that the greatest advances are often brought about through quite unspiritual drives. 'I saw,' says the author of Ecclesiastes, 'that all labour and all achievement spring from man's envy of his neighbour.' Or as the talmudic sages put it, 'Were it not for the evil inclination, no one would build a house, marry a wife, have children, or engage in business.' Purity of heart was essential to the relationship between man and God. But in relations between man and man, what mattered was the result, not the sentiment with which it was brought about. Jews would find it easy to agree with the remark of Sir James Frazer that 'it is better for the world that men should be right from wrong motives than that they would do wrong with the best intentions'.[8]

In general, then, the rabbis favoured markets and competition because they generated wealth, lowered prices, increased choice, reduced absolute levels of poverty, and in the course of time extended humanity's control over the environment, narrowing the extent to which we are the passive victims of circumstance and

---

[6] Adam Smith, *An Inquiry into the Nature and Causes of the Wealth of Nations*, New York: Modern Library, 1937, p. 14.

[7] Smith, *ibid.*, p. 423.

[8] Quoted in Hayek, *The Fatal Conceit, op. cit.*, p. 157.

fate. Competition releases energy and creativity and serves the general good. Admittedly, Jewish law permitted protectionist policies in some cases to safeguard the local economy, especially when the outside trader did not pay taxes. There were also times when rabbinic authorities intervened to lower prices of essential commodities. But in general they favoured the free market, nowhere more so than in their own professional sphere of Jewish education. An established teacher could not object to a rival setting up in competition. The reason they gave for this ruling illustrates their general approach. They said simply, 'Jealousy among scholars increases wisdom'.

Needless to say, in a faith as strongly moral as Judaism, alongside the respect for markets went a sharp insistence on the ethics of business. At one of the critical points of the Jewish calendar, on the Sabbath before the Ninth of Av when we recall the destruction of the two Temples, we read in the synagogue the great first chapter of Isaiah with its insistence that without political and economic integrity, religious piety is in vain:

'Seek justice, encourage the oppressed,
Defend the cause of the fatherless,
Plead the case of the widow . . .
Your silver has become dross,
Your choice wine is diluted with water,
Your rulers are rebels, companions of thieves,
They all love bribes and chase after gifts.'

The same message is carried through into the teachings of the rabbis. According to Rava, when a person comes to the next world for judgement, the first question he is asked is: Did you deal honestly in business? In the school of Rabbi Ishmael it was taught that whoever conducts himself honestly in business is as if he fulfilled the whole of Jewish law. The perennial temptations of the market – to pursue gain at someone else's expense, to take advantage of ignorance, to treat employees with indifference – needed to be fought against. Canons of fair trading had to be established and policed, and much of Jewish law is taken up with these concerns. The rabbis recognised that a perfect market would not emerge of its own accord. Not everyone had access to full information, and this gave scope for unscrupulous practices and unfair profits, against which they took a strong stand.

Perhaps the best summary of the way Judaism differed from Christianity, at least in its pre-Reformation guise, was given by Michael Novak, himself a Catholic:

> 'In both its prophetic and rabbinic traditions Jewish thought has always felt comfortable with a certain well-ordered worldliness, whereas the Christian has always felt a pull toward otherworldliness. Jewish thought has had a candid orientation toward private property, commercial activity, markets, and profits, whereas Catholic thought – articulated from an early period chiefly among priests and monks – has persistently tried to direct the attention of its adherents beyond the activities and interests of this world to the next.'[9]

So much, then, by way of an overview of Jewish economic ethics, much of which bears a strong kinship with views Hayek tirelessly espoused. But it is just here that I want to enter into the spirit of *The Fatal Conceit*, in which Hayek warned us to look, not just at markets, but also at the moral environment in which they are sustained. I want to draw attention briefly to five features of Judaism, essential to its way of life, which on the face of it stand utterly opposed to the market ethic.

The *first*, of course, is the Sabbath and its related institutions, the sabbatical year and the jubilee. The Sabbath is the boundary Judaism draws around economic activity. 'Six days shall you labour and do all your work, but the seventh day is a Sabbath to the Lord your God.' What marked the Sabbath off from all other religious celebrations in the ancient world was its concept of a day of rest. So unintelligible was this to the writers of ancient Greece that they accused Jews of observing it merely out of laziness. But of course what was at the heart of the Sabbath was and is the idea that there are important truths about the human condition that cannot be accounted for in terms of work or economics. That Sabbath is the day on which we neither work nor employ others to do our work, on which we neither buy nor sell, in which all manipulation of nature for creative ends is forbidden, in which all hierarchies of power or wealth are suspended.

The Sabbath is one of those phenomena – incomprehensible from the outside – which you have to live in order to understand.

---

[9] Michael Novak, *This Hemisphere of Liberty*, Washington DC: AEI Press, 1992, p. 64.

For countless generations of Jews it was the still point in the turning world, the moment at which we renew our attachment to family and community, during which we live the truth that the world is not wholly ours to bend to our will but something given to us in trust to conserve for future generations, and in which the inequalities of a market economy are counterbalanced by a world in which money does not count, in which we are all equal citizens. The Jewish writer Achad Ha-am was surely correct when he said that more than the Jews have kept the Sabbath, the Sabbath has kept the Jews. It was and is the one day in seven in which we live out all those values which are in danger of being obscured in the daily rush of events; the day in which we stop making a living and learn instead simply how to live.

Secondly, consider marriage and the family. Judaism is one of the great familial traditions, and this despite the fact that in strict legal terms a Jewish marriage has the form of a contract; that Judaism has never prohibited divorce by mutual consent; and that it is quite relaxed about that modern development, the pre-nuptial agreement, and indeed sees it as a useful device in alleviating the stress of separation. The reason Judaism has often succeeded in sustaining strong marriages and families has little to do with the structure of Jewish marriage law, and a great deal to do with its ritual life, the way in which many of the supreme religious moments take place in the home as a dialogue between husband and wife, or between parents and children. Ultimately, Judaism saw marriage not as a contract but as the supreme example of a covenant, namely a commitment based not on mutual benefit but on mutual belonging, whose key value is fidelity, holding fast to one another especially during difficult times because you are part of who I am. The Jewish family survived because, in the graphic phrase of the sages, it was surrounded by 'a hedge of roses', an elaborate network of rituals that bound individuals together in a matrix of mutual giving that was utterly at odds with a market ethic.

Thirdly, consider education. I have already mentioned that Jewish law favours competition in the provision of teaching. What it did not do, however, was to leave access to education to the market and to the ability to pay. Even in the days of Moses, Jews were instructed to set the highest religious value on education – as one of our most famous prayers, taken from the book of Deuteronomy, puts it:

> 'You shall teach these things diligently to your children, speaking of them when you sit at home or travel on the way, when you lie down and when you rise up.'

And by the first century, Jews had constructed the world's first system of universal compulsory education, funded by collective taxation. Education, the life of the mind, an ability to follow a train of thought and see the alternative possibilities that give rise to argument, are essential features of Jewish spirituality, and ones to which everyone, however poor, must be given access.

Fourthly, the concept of property. I mentioned earlier that Judaism has a high regard for private property as an institution governing the relations between human beings. At the same time, though, governing the relationship between humanity and God, there has been an equal insistence that what we have, we do not unconditionally own. Ultimately everything belongs to God. What we have, we hold in trust. And there are conditions to that trust – or as the great Victorian Jew Sir Moses Montefiore put it, 'We are worth what we are willing to share with others'.[10]

The effect of this idea on Jewish society has been profound. I was recently at a ceremony to mark the opening of a new Jewish school in one of our provincial communities. The project had been made possible by the great generosity of one of the local members. Over dinner I leaned over to him to express my thanks for his gift. He said, without a moment's reflection, 'What else could I do? The money wasn't mine. God lent it to me, and I invested it as wisely as I could in the next generation.' That kind of unreflective response lies at the foundation of the long tradition of Jewish philanthropy and explains much of how Judaism has been able to encourage the creation of wealth without giving rise to class resentments.

And finally, there is the Jewish tradition of law itself. It was a non-Jew, William Rees-Mogg, who first drew my attention to the connection between Jewish law and the control of inflation, a link that I confess I never thought of making. His argument is

---

[10] Lawrence J. Epstein, *A Treasury of Jewish Anecdotes*, New Jersey: Jason Aronson, 1989, p. 162.

contained in a book he wrote during an era of high inflation (in 1974), entitled *The Reigning Error*.[11] It was simply this. 'Inflation is a disease of inordinacy.' It comes about through a failure to understand that energy, to be channelled, needs restraints. It was the constant discipline of law, he says, that provided the boundaries within which Jewish creativity could flow. The law, to quote his words:

'has acted as a bottle inside which this spiritual and intellectual energy could be held; only because it could be held has it been possible to make use of it. It has not merely exploded or been dispersed; it has been harnessed as a continuous power.'

Jews, for him, were a model of acquired self-restraint, and it was the failure of societies to practice self-restraint that led to runaway inflation.

And with this I come back to Hayek and *The Fatal Conceit*. It was Hayek's view that moral systems produced their results, not directly or by conscious intention, but rather in the long run and often in ways that could not have been foreseen. Certainly Jews believed that their way of life would lead to the blessings of prosperity. That, after all, is the substance of many of Moses's prophecies. But there was no direct connection between institutions like the Sabbath and economic growth. How could there be? The Sabbath, the family, the educational system, the concept of ownership as trusteeship, and the disciplines of the law, were not constructed on the basis of economic calculation. To the contrary, they were ways in which Judaism in effect said to the market: thus far and no further. There are realms in which you may not intrude.

The concept of the holy is precisely the domain in which the worth of things is not judged by their market price or economic value. And this fundamental insight of Judaism is all the more striking given its respect for the market within the market-place. *The Fatal Conceit* for Judaism, as for Hayek, is to believe that the market governs the totality of our lives, when it in fact governs only a limited part of it, that which concerns goods which we think of as being subject to production and exchange. There are things

---

[11] William Rees-Mogg, *The Reigning Error*, London: Hamish Hamilton, 1974.

fundamental to being human that we do not produce; instead we receive from those who came before us and from God Himself. And there are things which we may not exchange, however high the price.

What then might be the lesson of *The Fatal Conceit* for our time? That socialism is not the only enemy of the market economy. Another enemy, all the more powerful for its recent global triumph, is the market economy itself. When everything that matters can be bought and sold, when commitments can be broken because they are no longer to our advantage, when shopping becomes salvation and advertising slogans become our litany, when our worth is measured by how much we earn and spend, then the market is destroying the very virtues on which in the long run it depends. That, not the return of socialism, is the danger that advanced economies now face. And at such times as now, when markets seem to hold out the promise of uninterrupted growth in our satisfaction of desires, the voice of our great religious traditions needs to be heard, warning us of the gods that devour their own children, and of the temples that stand today as relics of civilisations that once seemed invincible.

The market, in my view, has already gone too far: not indeed as an economic system, but as a cast of thought governing relationships and the image we have of ourselves. A great rabbi once taught this lesson to a successful but unhappy businessman. He took him to the window and asked him, What do you see? The man replied, I see the world. He then took him to a mirror and asked, What do you see? He replied, I see myself. That, said the rabbi, is what happens when silver covers glass. Instead of seeing the world you see only yourself. The idea that human happiness can be exhaustively accounted for in terms of things we can buy, exchange and replace, is one of the great corrosive acids which eats away the girders on which societies rest; and by the time we have discovered this, it is already too late.

Hayek's final contribution to the great debate about economic systems was to remind us that the market does not survive by market forces alone. It depends on respect for institutions, which are themselves expressions of our reverence for the human individual as the image and likeness of God.

Further Reading

F.A.Hayek, *The Constitution of Liberty*, London: Routledge & Kegan Paul, 1960.

—, *The Road to Serfdom*, London: Routledge & Kegan Paul, 1971.

Michael Novak, *This Hemisphere of Liberty*, Washington DC: AEI Press, 1992.

—, *The Spirit of Democratic Capitalism*, London: IEA Health and Welfare Unit, 1991.

—, *The Catholic Ethic and the Spirit of Capitalism*, New York: The Free Press, 1993.

Jonathan Sacks, *The Politics of Hope*, London: Jonathan Cape, 1997.

—, 'Wealth and Poverty: a Jewish Analysis', in *Tradition in an Untraditional Age*, London: Vallentine Mitchell, 1990.

The Market Still Inadequate?
Professor Norman Barry
University of Buckingham

THE CHIEF RABBI, DR JONATHAN SACKS, has given us an intriguing and provocative survey of the current state of thinking about the moral status of the market. It is all the more instructive because it is written from the perspective of someone whose high intellectual and moral authority in the Jewish faith is unquestioned and yet one who also evinces an intimate knowledge of the social thought of the writer, F. A. Hayek, who is celebrated in this lecture. Dr Sacks has the requisite philosophical and economic knowledge of the tradition of thought of which that writer was so distinguished a representative. However, Dr Sacks's approach is not that of an uncritical admirer of the market system; his lecture reveals the reflections of someone who has thought deeply about the weaknesses as well as the strengths of the doctrine of liberal economics, and the social system it describes.

He belongs to what we might loosely call the 'market is not enough' tradition of liberalism (using that word in the European, not the American, sense). His target, though unnamed, is probably the Chicago neo-reductionist school of economics, whose adherents believe that most of our considerations on social affairs can be encompassed in the economic calculus. Dr Sacks does not think that the socialists, or any other kind of political interventionists, have anything to teach us about economics, but rather that liberal political economy does not capture all that we understand by 'civil society' and, furthermore, he believes that the very survival of the free economic order depends upon its embrace of values which are irreducible to economics. The market is not self-sufficient and its fragile moral basis needs constant replenishment from non-economic sources. Not surprisingly, Dr Sacks shows, in stimulating detail, how so worldly and pro-market a religion as Judaism recognised that its believers needed something in addition to the knowledge provided by the price system if they were to fulfil the moral promise of their faith.

I shall question this alleged moral deficiency of free-market economics from two different but related intellectual positions. *First*, I shall defend the idea that exchange develops its own rules and conventions so that the market system does not depend for its validity on any outside source, such as religion or indeed, moral philosophy. *Second*, as a purely practical point, I would like to suggest that the admission of morality into the language of the market, which has now become something of a fad, produces deleterious consequences for capitalism. A glance at recent history tells us why.

No group of people is more anxious to stress the moral failure of the market (while reluctantly acknowledging its allocative efficiency) than the erstwhile socialists. Indeed, an academic discipline called 'business ethics'[1] has been invented which subjects business to some kind of external moral audit, success at which would more likely result in rapid business failure than moral enlightenment. Most of its prescriptions constitute socialism by another name. An early practical example of my case was Germany: the economic rigour of post-war German Ordoliberalism (to which Erhard owed his intellectual allegiance) was gradually softened, and eventually neutered, by the influence of the morally-inspired 'Social Market Economy', with the malign results of which Germany is still struggling. I do not mean to suggest that Dr Sacks has any sympathy with these aberrations but only that they have been made possible by allowing 'external' morality, or some modern socialistically-inclined religions, too much of an influence in the explanation and defence of markets.

But, first, I should like to put my own elaboration and interpretation of the true things that Dr Sacks says about religion and the market. If we look at the history of the great religions in the world we find more than just a weary acceptance of the market but actually a positive approval of its efficiency and freedom-enhancing properties. The foundations of classical economics were laid down a long time before Adam Smith and the Scottish Enlightenment celebrated the price and private property systems.

---

[1] For a critique, see Norman Barry, *Business Ethics*, London: Macmillan, 1998.

The School of Salamanca,[2] Jesuit priests in 16th-century Spain, had already discovered the quantity theory of money, defined the 'just' price in terms of efficiency rather than morality, and elaborated on all the other features of micro-economics except the margin. Catholic natural law (including the original prohibition against usury) proved no intellectual barrier against market capitalism. But even before this, Islamic scholars (especially Kaldhun, the 13th-century historian) had demonstrated that the Koran encouraged private property, entrepreneurship and incredibly low taxation. As with Catholicism, a proper understanding of Islam showed that the prohibition of the Riba, or usurious rate of interest, did not outlaw most normal market rates.

Dr Sacks is right to stress that the key to the success of market economies is their capacity to combine the features of entrepreneurship (individual flair and the capability for discovery and innovation) with respect for tradition, most often based on religion. But tradition is not some mystical quality, a transcendental belief system to be revered for no human reason or practical interest, as some conservatives seem to think, but it is in a prudential sense linked to the utilitarian value of predictable rules. Market traders need these more than anything else and tradition, exemplified by the common law, has been a better source of predictability and stability than any designed legal code.

From Dr Sacks's own description, Judaism is a splendidly practical religion; the roots of it are biblical but its practices and prescriptions are securely fastened to men's needs. With the exception (as always) of a few American intellectuals, its believers are solidly pro-market. This affection seems primarily to arise from the biblical respect for property, economic independence and a conception of individualism that makes personal striving for freedom and autonomy perfectly compatible with the irresistible pull of family and communal obligations. This is not the *ersatz* communitarianism of late 20th-century rootless intellectuals in search of a creed but the live doctrine of compelling but not coerced social duties. Furthermore, Dr Sacks has a quite evocative page referring to the duty of Judaism (as of all religions) to tame

---

[2] Marjorie Grice-Hutchinson, *The School of Salamanca*, Oxford: The Clarendon Press, 1952.

nature for the benefit of man ('...to fill the earth and subdue it', p. 16): it is compulsory reading for environmentalists who recommend that we should lie down supine before a pristine nature and sacrifice our human interests for the latest threatened species that happens to catch the moral vanity of the conservationist. Judaism sees no virtue in poverty.

Again, the business ethics (I hate to call it that) of Judaism seem eminently practical. There is none of the moral pretentiousness, and commercial naivety, of those who would urge the 'social responsibility of the corporation' or make business the bearers of the costs of the latest fashion of political philosophy and supererogatory morality; but instead there is the less glamorous emphasis on the more mundane but absolutely necessary virtues of honesty, fair dealing, respect for contract and property, and the refusal to exploit egoistically and egregiously those informational asymmetries that often occur in business life. The problem here is that modern ethicists have transformed the perfectly sensible requests for transparency and honesty in business into strident and economically counterproductive demands for level playing fields in stock markets and pleas for the elimination of any (apparently) correctable inequality in market transactions.

Yet it is in this Jewish tradition where Dr Sacks finds the source for his scepticism about the adequacy of the morality of markets. In a section which I found less than convincing, he discusses five features of Jewish life that are rooted in apparently anti-free market values but which are nevertheless essential for the preservation of the Jewish tradition and community. He singles out the sanctity of the Sabbath (which, he says, expresses in a symbolic and practical way religious phenomena not accounted for by work and economics); ideals of family and marriage which are protected from the potential ravages of individual choice, despite Jewish marriage law being based on contract (and not on an unbreakable vow); tax-funded education; a communalised concept of property (it is held in trust); and a belief in fixed and unchangeable law (especially with regard to the currency).

I cannot see how these prescriptions (with the possible exception of tax-funded education) are antithetical to the market; most of them (especially the last) cohere perfectly well with the disciplines that the exchange system has gradually produced and are consistent with the completed *telos* of a free society, which surely does approve of some non-profit or non-market driven choices. Even communalised property can be made consistent with the free choices of the property-holders. The classical liberal objects only when non-market strategies (such as religious conformity) are coerced. Indeed, what kind of moral value does the Sabbath have where it is sustained only by law?

Marriage is a particularly instructive example for Jews and non-Jews alike, for the destruction of marriage and the family in the USA and Britain has not occurred because the marital union, based on the permanence of the vow, has been replaced by the free choice of contract but because in these jurisdictions it is founded on nothing more lasting than the ephemeral allure of romance. Fault has been all but eliminated from divorce proceedings and the wrongdoer in a breach of marital trust is the one most likely to walk off with the spoils. Modern marriage involves a 'contract' which is significantly less demanding than that involved in house purchase. In fact, it is no contract at all precisely because the law imposes no penalty on those who breach it.

In his critique of the free market, I think Dr Sacks has in mind the instigators of the perversions of free market doctrine – welfare theorists and others who would eliminate the notion of responsibility from freedom are to blame for the familiar aberrations. Marriage is not the only example. The capture of the American legal system by tort lawyers (and the almost complete elimination of the idea that we take on responsibilities by contract) is another example of the all-pervading anti-market dogma that somebody else is always to blame for our own misfortunes (and, in Europe especially, the idea is held that the state must always rescue those who make mistakes by their own choices).

This brings me to the nub of Dr Sacks's qualifications to market individualism. He refers to Hayek's *The Fatal Conceit* in his argument against *laissez-faire* enthusiasts: they think that the market

> 'governs the totality of our lives, when it in fact governs only a limited part of it...goods... subject to production and exchange. There are things fundamental to being human that we do not produce; instead we receive from those who came before us and from God himself. And there are things which we may not exchange, however high the price'. (p. 23-24)

[31]

Dr Sacks is in a distinguished tradition of pro-market thinkers who shrink a little from the full implications of the theory and practice of the doctrine. Adam Smith had many doubts about the market system, none more famous than his fear that the division of labour would produce a stupid and alienated population incapable of grasping basic moral rules: this apparently grievous deficiency of the market (a gift for collectivists) required partially state-funded education. Other writers have suggested that the market cannot generate its own morality, it has to come in from the outside, as in Wilhelm Ropke's famous comment that:

'The market, competition and the play of supply and demand do not create ethical reserves; they presuppose and consume them. These reserves must come from outside the market...'[3]

This is now the conventional wisdom, but I think that it rests on a mistake. It is not understood often enough that the practice of trade itself generates those capacities of honesty and trust that the market needs. We do not have to know each other to follow these rules, least of all need we share the same religion or belong to the same race; we simply have to be regular participants in the practice of dealing and trading. We in effect play repeated games and this enables us to identify cheats, liars and non-co-operators. As David Hume (a much more astute observer of the market than Smith) noted, moral rules are simple *conventions* and though they are often sanctioned by a religion, which gives them a moral gloss that encourages obedience, their rationale is strictly human. Of the trading relationship between two farmers, Hume said:

'Your corn is ripe today; mine will be so tomorrow. 'Tis profitable for us both, that I should labour with you today, and that you should aid me tomorrow. I have no kindness, and know you have as little for me....Hence I learn to do a service to another, without any real kindness, because I foresee he will return my service...'[4]

It is true that we inherit rules which we did not choose (like we pick a new car or dress) and these moral legacies did not begin in

---

[3] Wilhelm Ropke, *A Humane Economy*, London: Wolf, 1960, p.125.

[4] David Hume, *A Treatise of Human Nature*, New York: Macmillan, 1948, Book III, pp. 61-62.

some 'social contract' but in social practice. But we accept them and we follow them precisely because they have utilitarian value. We abandon them if they fail to service the market, as the strict rules against usury were discarded. Again, perhaps there was a need to change the rules about environment protection because the common law of nuisance failed to deal adequately with modern conditions (though statute undoubtedly made things worse) but these movements do not represent any great moral change.

One of the great virtues of religions is that they tend to embody the moral rules that underlie the practices and conventions of the market and this is why the market has been seen to be consistent with a variety of faiths: they are compatible with its *generic* moral code. It is the fact that market practices service a minimalist conception of man, his moral capacity and his potentiality that is important, not the religions themselves that often underlie them. Thus I believe that Dr Sacks is profoundly mistaken when he says that:

> 'The idea that human happiness can be exhaustively accounted for in terms of things we can buy, exchange and replace is one of the great corrosive acids which eats away the girders on which societies rest; and by the time we have discovered this, it is already too late' (p. 24).

On the contrary, I believe that the achievement of commercial relationships is the key not only to prosperity but also to peace and contentment. And the conventions and injunctions on which the market rests – honour promises, respect property and take responsibility for actions – are just the most important of its demands. The 'corrosive acid' that eats away at the girders of liberty is still the state (especially its welfare system), for it is government, with its abrogation of the principles and market conventions which I have just outlined, that has systematically attenuated individual responsibility.

Ironically, it is not consumerism and wild, unconstrained free choice which are threatening the viability of established traditions, but 'morality' itself; and here I refer to considerably less sophisticated moralists than Dr Sacks. For the moral activist is intuitively opposed to markets (they do not gel with his highest moral convictions). But now that he is compelled to accept them he is determined that they should be 'cabin'd, cribbed and confin'd' by ethics. The 'social market', communitarian capitalism, and equal market opportunities are the kinds of distortions which contemporary morality threatens to bequeath to a future capitalist generation. Individuals may trade but only under the licence of the moralist. I am sure that Dr Sacks would approve of little of this but once an expansive morality is allowed to penetrate market relationships, which are already based on reliable conventions, I can see no means for restricting its domain.

People only created the free society by breaking out of the confines of traditional rules and practices (something that Hayek found hard to explain).[5] It would be tragic if similar constraints were reintroduced by the design of professors of moral philosophy. None of this is meant to devalue the importance of a minimalist morality but only to keep it in its place. I, for one, do not know of any free society that was 'corroded' by too much buying and selling – as long as the buyers were using their own money and the sellers were offering goods they had not stolen. But like Mandeville, I think of the bees whose prosperity, hard work and sociability degenerated into quarrels and fractiousness once they 'got morality'.

---

[5] Norman Barry, 'Hayek's Theory of Social Order', *Il Politico*, 1996.

Markets and Morals: A Personal View
Professor Robert Davidson
University of Glasgow, 1972-91

IN HIS 1998 IEA HAYEK MEMORIAL LECTURE, DR JONATHAN SACKS provides an incisive and illuminating critique of Friedrich Hayek's *The Fatal Conceit*. He focuses especially on Hayek's reflections on the role religion played in shaping and preserving the moral traditions which were essential before the market economy could be sustained. It is a critique made, not surprisingly, from the standpoint of orthodox Judaism. That is its strength and also its limitations. My purpose is to try and take some of Dr Sacks's insights and place them in a wider context.

Dr Sacks has little difficulty in showing how, starting out from a biblical base, Jews and Judaism found that free enterprise and trade offered them a congenial economic framework. Jewish tradition, however, also contains within itself elements which clearly say to the market economy 'thus far, and no further'. Among these elements he lists: the Sabbath, marriage and the family, education which does not depend on the ability to pay, property which is not unconditionally owned, and the tradition of law which demands self-restraint, the failure to practise which may lead to runaway inflation. It is the interplay between these two facets of Jewish tradition that I wish to explore on a wider canvas. His concluding reflections, indeed, are an invitation to such an exploration:

> 'The market, in my view, has already gone too far: not indeed as an economic system, but as a cast of thought governing relationships and the image we have of ourselves...The idea that human happiness can be exhaustively accounted for in terms of things we can buy, exchange and replace, is one of the great corrosive acids which eats away the girders on which societies rest; and by the time we have discovered this, it is already too late.' (p. 24)

His final words are to remind us, following Hayek, that 'the market does not survive by market forces alone. It depends on respect for institutions, which are themselves expressions of our reverence for the human individual as the image and likeness of God'. But what precisely are these institutions and the religious traditions which they express, and what do they guarantee or achieve?

It is ironic that in the course of discussing Hayek's view, following Edmund Burke and Max Weber, that only certain kinds of society give rise to, and are capable of sustaining, a market economy, Dr Sacks comments:

> 'The answer which each of them gave – an answer that has been given new salience by the rise of the economies of South East Asia – is that they tend to be societies with a strong respect for certain kinds of tradition.' (p. 11)

Even if the argument holds that it is certain kinds of strongly held traditions which give rise to such economies, the recent collapse of the markets in Japan and South Korea, triggering off the fear of a global recession, hardly gives convincing reasons to believe that such traditions can *sustain* a market economy or prevent such an economy from being vulnerable to other factors. Indeed, there may be elements in the traditions which feed the collapse of the market economy or raise fundamental questions about its long-term viability. It may be argued, for example, that the Japanese cast of mind, moulded by centuries of tradition, while brilliantly successful in certain areas, did not have within it the flexibility to respond quickly enough to new factors in the global economy.

Traditions are seldom monolithic or static. They are complex organisms which contain within themselves disparate elements, often in tension with one another, elements which respond to changing social and cultural factors. This is true of Judaism with its richly varied expressions today, ranging all the way from Progressive and Liberal to Conservative and Orthodox. Other traditions confront us with the same spectrum, not least Christianity in its different denominational and global expressions. Let us take two of the five features of Judaism which Dr Sacks rightly sees as being opposed to market ethics.

The Sabbath, which he memorably describes as 'the day in which we stop making a living and learn instead simply how to live' (p. 21). The 'we' in this statement, and in relationship to the

Sabbath ritual, can be no other than the members of the Jewish community, but there are many Jews today whose celebration of the Sabbath leaves much to be desired in terms of traditional Jewish practice and others who sit very lightly to it. Its Christian counterpart, transferred to Sunday, the day of the resurrection of Jesus, sought for centuries, and still does in certain expressions of faith, to preserve the same basic insight. Yet Sunday today has undergone a dramatic transformation. Economic factors and social conditions have ensured that Sunday is no longer the traditional day of rest. For some this is a matter of choice, for others a matter of economic necessity. The supermarkets and the cinemas are open. Football matches are increasingly being transferred from Saturday to Sunday. No amount of protest from the Lord's Day Observance Society or from the Save Our Sunday movement is going to reconstitute the traditional Sunday. If there are values, important values, which it sought to preserve, in what form can these values survive in the rapidly changing society in which we live, and in a world in which powerful economic forces control many of the changes?

Marriage and the family. The central significance given to marriage and the family within Judaism and within Christian tradition has traditionally never been in doubt. There are powerful reasons for this. As Dr Sacks pertinently comments, after setting marriage within the context of Jewish ritual:

> 'Ultimately, Judaism saw marriage not as a contract, but as the supreme example of a covenant, namely a commitment based not on mutual benefit but on mutual belonging, whose key value is fidelity, holding fast to one another especially during difficult times because you are part of who I am.' (p. 21)

There are, however, many people today who are asserting and proving in practice that this key value of fidelity can be a reality in relationships other than the traditional marriage bond, relationships both heterosexual and homosexual. Equally, while divorce by mutual consent has always been recognised in the Jewish community, the current rate of divorce in society raises serious questions about the validity of the traditional marriage ethos.

It may be rightly claimed that the Sabbath and marriage are

opposed to market ethics, but are such traditional values doomed to become the hallmark of a religious minority struggling to survive and progressively driven to adapt to market forces over which they have no control?

Let us consider the immediate impact which market forces have, for better or for worse, on parts of the traditions which have nurtured society. Take two out of the many examples which highlight the problem.

First, when two years ago the American-based electronic company Viasystems took over a factory in the Scottish border town of Selkirk, it did so in a fanfare of publicity, inviting the workforce to buy sunglasses since the future was so bright. Eighteen months later the redundancy notices were issued. The factory was closing. It was not that the factory was a failure. It had a skilled workforce and the productivity was high. It contributed to the increased profits which the company achieved world-wide during that period. Yet the factory was sacrificed on the altar of a move to another site within the UK where more substantial government assistance was now on offer. The closure was made purely on financial grounds, the prospect of a larger financial contribution to an already highly profitable multinational company. What was not taken into account was the devastating effect the closure would have on the local community: on skilled workers for whom there was no alternative employment, on young people whose hopes of employment had been dashed and who saw in the closure another nail in the coffin of a dying community, on families where often more than one wage earner depended on the factory, on many small local businesses whose viability depended on the money generated within the community by a high tech business. The whole social fabric of the community was under threat; its viability as a living community embracing young and old was called into question. Confidence in the future was replaced by fear and a gnawing sense of hopelessness. Increasing tensions were generated within family life.

When confronted with a market economy increasingly dominated by multinational companies, the appeal for wealth to be handled responsibly in the interests of the community which contributes to such wealth tends to fall on deaf ears, if the company decides there are richer pickings to be had elsewhere. If

[38]

wealth exists, as Jewish tradition insists, to promote human wellbeing, what restraints can that, or any religious or moral tradition, exercise in such a situation, or is it totally powerless, while many of the values which it fosters in community and family life are under threat?

Or take the broader picture in this country. In the last 20 years millions of what were once regarded as secure shopfloor factory jobs have disappeared, to be replaced in many cases by service industry jobs, many of them part time, poorly paid and offering no long-term security. Such restructuring of the workforce may be inevitable, its inevitability spelled out by market forces, but have we counted the cost in terms of the social fabric of society? What happens, for example, to family life, when both parents are forced to go out to work at different hours to part-time jobs, just to make ends meet and to provide for the basic food and clothing needs of the family? What happens to the self-esteem of a university graduate who can see no future beyond a part-time job in a bar? These are not theoretical cases; they are only too tragically common in society today.

Second, in his discussion of David Landes's *The Wealth and Poverty of Nations,*[6] Dr Sacks identifies Judaism as

'the religion of a people born in slavery and longing for redemption; and the great assault of slavery against human dignity is that it deprives me of the wealth I create. At the heart of the Hebrew Bible is the God who seeks the free worship of free human beings, and two of the most powerful defences of freedom are private property and economic independence'. (p. 14-15)

But what does this mean in a world controlled by economic forces which ensure that for countless millions of people today 'the ownership of the wealth I create' and 'economic independence' are impossible dreams as they live with the consequences of debt slavery?

When dramatic tragedy strikes such people, as it did in Central America with hurricane Mitch, individuals and nations across the world respond generously with immediately needed aid in goods and in money, to begin the long process of rebuilding the

---

6   David Landes, *The Wealth and Poverty of Nations, op. cit.*

infrastructure of devastated communities. Before hurricane Mitch struck, however, life for many people in Nicaragua was a daily struggle to survive. The average income per person was £250 per annum, while £750 per person was being annually paid to service debts owed to international banks and to the IMF. The net result of this imbalance on the country's infrastructure, on the provision of education, of medical facilities and of the social services we take as our right, needs no underlining.

We may, we must analyse the reasons for, and attribute responsibility for such a debt crisis, but that should not blind us to the fact that it has arisen in the context of market forces from which some of us benefit, but which have left the lives of countless people blighted. Where stand our traditional values in the world in which a UN Report has estimated that debt relief could save the lives of 26 million children by the year 2000?

All this is but the tip of an iceberg. There are many other issues facing us today on a global scale in which there is a direct or potential conflict between unfettered market forces and other values. Environmentalists, for example, rightly direct our attention to the dangers that we pose to the sustainability of our natural habitat, because of exploitation or production methods which are market driven. The Judeo-Christian tradition of creation has something to contribute to this issue. And what of the ethics of Western tobacco companies distributing free Western cigarettes in China, where smoking-related diseases are increasing at an alarming rate?

Theologians and religious leaders, of course, have no more right to tell economists what economic theory they ought to espouse than economists have to dogmatise on religious traditions, yet a society without some agreed set of values is like a ship drifting aimlessly. It is this sense of aimlessness and indeed hopelessness, which seems to characterise so many people today. For many there seems to be no light at the end of the dark tunnel of homelessness, unemployment and drug abuse. It must be the task of the theologian, working within his or her religious traditional framework, to point people to some vision of hope, as it must be the task of the religious communities to bear witness to such a vision in the way they order their lives.

Visions, however, can be illusory or impractical. An appeal to inflexible traditional values may be neither appropriate nor helpful. A society, however, without some vision can be a cold, cruel place which serves the interests of the few and leaves the many without hope. Vision must be tested against reality. As has been wisely said:

> 'Does it help us to see the world as it is, and as it will be or might be more clearly? Does it enable and encourage hopeful, courageous, just and loving behaviour? Does it (that is vision) help us to see evil, oppression and injustice for what they are, even if we benefit from them, and to respond to them with faithful steadfastness? Above all, does it challenge and enable us to do justice, and to love kindness and to walk humbly with our God?'[7]

---

[7] D .B. Forrester, *Christian Justice and Public Policy*, Cambridge: Cambridge University Press, 1997, p. 259.

What the World Owes Judaism

Professor Michael Novak

American Enterprise Institute, Washington DC

FRIEDRICH HAYEK WAS ONE OF THOSE PERSONS who recognised the importance of religion, even for economics, while confessing that he himself had no ear for it. The Chief Rabbi takes up Hayek's challenge and points to the crucial role that Judaism plays in the culture that supports economic liberty. In these remarks, I would like to expand his remarks in order to express gratitude to Judaism for its contributions to political liberty, as well.

It must first be remarked, though, that there is more than one Jewish tradition, just as there is more than one Christian tradition. Thus, to speak of 'Judaeo-Christian tradition' is doubly mistaken; it suggests both a singular tradition and a syncretistic one, at that. To speak of 'Jewish-Christian traditions', while perhaps acceptable, runs the risk of doing less than adequate justice to Judaism as it is in itself, by reflecting on it, rather, through the lens of Christian history. I must confess that, in what follows, I am writing as a Christian, and reflecting on those elements in Christian culture that Christians derive from Judaism. This approach risks ringing a little false to Jews – not quite on target, not quite accurate to the Jewish experience in itself. It is, nonetheless, what one Christian recognises as his indebtedness to Judaism, even if the lessons learned are (from a Jewish point of view) much too coloured by Christian filters. I can only hope the effort furthers mutual amity and is, however faulty, a useful first step.

The influence of Judaism has never depended upon mere numbers. Today's sceptic may object that of the world's 5.5 billion people, about two billion are Christian, just under one billion are Muslim, and there are only 13 million Jews. But that would be to miss a crucial point. The truth of Christianity presupposes the truth of Judaism; indeed, Christianity is not really intelligible apart from Judaism. (This relation is asymmetrical since the truth of Judaism does not presuppose Christianity.) Islam, too, considers itself an Abrahamic religion. Thus, the significance of Judaism is felt throughout the world not only directly but also through the religions descended from it. These include most humans who address God as Creator, Governor of history and Judge.

Through its understanding of the One God, Lord of all history, Judaism ruptured the self-enclosed cycles of archaic Time, as repetitive as the motions of the spheres, which dominated the imagination of the Greeks, Romans and peoples of the East. Judaism shattered this cyclical view with a conception of history, narrative and progress – of Time as a story with a beginning, middle and end, intelligible to its Creator, loved in its entirety by Him, and presided over by Him as its gracious Governor and undeceivable Judge. Judaism, in short, gave history (and human destiny) a point, and thus a conception of progress. This conception, in turn, grounded our modern sense of personal responsibility and personal meaningfulness.

Judaism taught that the reason for all the galaxies and stars, the motions of the heavens and the vastnesses of space was this: So that there would be in this largely silent universe at least one creature made in the image of God, and capable of insight and choice. Such a creature could become conscious of what God had wrought, be moved by God's greatness and His love, and 'in the fear of the Lord', give thanks.

Rabbi Sacks stresses the importance of the Jewish trust in the final goodness of creation, especially in regard to economics. Concurring in this emphasis, I wish to draw out two further implications, the first as regards the possibility of civilised discourse, the second as regards the work of science.

John Adams, the second president of the United States, wrote that even if he were an atheist, he would believe that the Hebrews were the single most important people to the future course of civilisation. Why? Because the Hebrews had introduced into history the conception of a single Creator and a single Judge. This conviction introduced into history the conception of truth, a truth that springs from the understanding of God. One implication – everything that is, is intelligible to its Maker. The Creator of all things understands them all, and He loves the whole, as well. If we pursue the evidence uncovered by our own eros of inquiry, we may rightly hold high expectations that that inquiry will not be in vain.

This belief, as Alfred Lord Whitehead was later to remark,[1] having nourished the human race for five thousand years, made the eventual rise of modern science possible. Apart from this belief, the rise of science would have been highly unlikely – for the Hebrew God is a God of particulars, contingents and singulars, not solely the God of unchanging universals. Thus, the modern reliance on probabilities and emergent patterns of new probabilities in an open universe seemed quite plausible, once it took shape.

Yet another implication of the point made by President Adams was the possibility of civilised discourse. If the world is intelligible to its Creator and Judge, then there is a right and a wrong, and human beings should be able to explore each facet of creation in order to discern evidence concerning which opinions about it are true or false. Every person, therefore, is held to standards of evidence. In the aphorism of St Thomas Aquinas: civilisation is constituted by conversation. Civilised people reason together, argue, offer reasons, pay one another the respect due other rational creatures. Barbarians club one another. Standards of evidence make civilisation possible ('and the truth shall make you free'), just as their avoidance brings it to ruin.

By its convictions about the Creator, therefore, Judaism rooted our political and economic liberties in fidelity to truth. But Judaism has also made other contributions of great importance to the free society. Let me mention only three of them: the contributions of its sexual teaching; its emphasis on creativity; and its understanding that one definition of true religion emphasises compassion for the widow, the fatherless, and the stranger (see Deuteronomy 10:18f and *passim*).

On sexual teaching, Judaism was unique among all the religions then prominent in the Mediterranean basin. Judaism taught that 'male and female He made them', and 'in His image He made them' (Genesis 1). In other words, something about the union between male and female is the point within creation that best

---

[1] *Science and the Modern World*, New York, 1948, pp. 12-13.

reveals the nature of the Creator Himself. There is something especially sacred, especially God-like, in the union of male and female. Thus, from the beginning, the priests of Judaism found temple prostitution and other common practices of the pagan religions of their region abominable. Judaism also distinguished itself, while especially privileging the sexual relationship between male and female, by rejecting sexual commerce between persons of the same sex. The moral, political and economic results of this historic transvaluation of sexual values has been dramatic.

On the one hand, Jewish sexual teaching placed the family at the very centre of civilised life. Judaism's special conception of the proper sexual relations between male and female added a new kind of dignity both to the man and to the woman. It conferred on the woman a status equal to that of the male, as a person to be respected and cherished in her own right. And it demanded of the male considerable restraint, self-control and discipline. Among Jews and Christians was later born the idea that the highest and most beautiful of all friendships is the friendship between man and woman in matrimony.

From this ideal, plus the struggles implied by the chastity required for monogamous love, was born the heresy – a popular heresy – that Denis de Rougemont called 'the myth of romantic love'.[2] This errant passion, an escape from realistic love and permanent commitment ('for better or worse'), inspires the uniquely Western plot line of most of our dramatic art, from *The Song of Roland* to *Romeo and Juliet, Anna Karenina* to a slough of Hollywood romances, and usually ends in self-destruction.

Historical experience has shown that a civilisation based on monogamous family ties gains political and economic strength not found in any other social formation. Through the family, economic activities gain cumulative weight over time. As an economic unit, the family gives ground for one generation to labour with considerable self-sacrifice for the betterment of the next, and so on down the generations.

In a parallel fashion, as the elemental living cell of the free society, family life teaches its members a certain practical realism, a sense of honesty, and mutual acceptance (including mutual

---

[2] *Passion and Society*, trans. Montgomery Belgion, London: Faber and Faber, 1940.

forgiveness). Such habits are of enormous importance to the public life of free societies. The ordinary self-sacrifice the family teaches its members, as well as the radical honesty it teaches them to express one to the other, have always been a threat to totalitarian leaders – that is one reason such leaders have historically treated the family ruthlessly. Such radical honesty in family life is one of the great sources of practical realism and moral heroism in the free society. (Hence the advice for young people: If you do not like honesty, avoid marriage. In matrimony, you will bind yourself to a person who feels obliged to tell you all the things you do not really want to hear about yourself. That is not entirely pleasant, but it is good for your soul.)

Then there is the emphasis on creativity. In imagining God as the Creator of all things, and the human being as created in His image, Judaism has taught the world that it is not enough for each of us merely to be passive; in some sense, it is our obligation to work for justice and righteousness. This obligation is *not* identical to what Hayek called 'the fatal conceit', that is, the error of 'constructivism', the error of thinking that society is like a machine that we can take apart and put together at will. On the contrary, this obligation induces the profound sense that by hard thought and sacrifice we can help to put our children in a better position than the one in which we began, and that thus we can make a contribution towards building a more decent society, one family at a time. This is an important creative task, but also a humble and realistic one. It is a task essential for the future prospects of any free and self-governing society.

The former Librarian of Congress, Daniel Boorstin, in the second book in his trilogy on human achievement, *The Creators*,[3] recounts being surprised to find that the roots of the ideal of creativity have a religious basis that is practically unique to Judaism (and, following it, Christianity).

In his recent huge study, *The Wealth and Poverty of Nations*,[4] Harvard's David Landes also amasses a great deal of evidence for the superior economic achievements over time of European and

---

[3] New York: Random House, 1993.

[4] David Landes, *The Wealth and Poverty of Nations*, New York: W. W. Norton & Company, 1998.

[47]

North American civilisations, as compared with other great civilisations in history. He attributes the striking creation of wealth in this civilisation, sustained over time, to three characteristics, which each go back to Judaism: Jewish-Christian respect for manual labour; the Jewish-Christian subordination of nature to humankind; and the Jewish-Christian sense of time as a narrative, going somewhere (linear, not circular), progressive. He then places his greatest stress on two further features of Jewish-Christian civilisation: the prominence given the market (a relatively free market), and the importance given creativity and innovation.

In the third place, Judaism taught the human race that true religion is measured by compassion. The measure of progress in any society is its concern for the poorest and most vulnerable of its members. This teaching ensures that human beings should regard all other human beings as part of the same common project. Drawing on this preconscious tradition, for instance, Adam Smith – to my way of thinking, one of the greatest figures in the entire history of the British Isles, and the greatest of all revolutionaries in the project of raising up the poor of the world – called his book not 'The Wealth of Individuals', but *The Wealth of Nations*. His was a pre-eminently *social* view, and his book was aimed at inspiring human beings to work for a world in which the burdens of poverty would be lifted from every individual on the planet. This great social project, Smith knew, would take time, but the point of his pioneering inquiry was to learn the nature and causes of the wealth of nations, and to put them into practice in a systematic way, in order to better the condition of the entire human race. He dreamed, he said, of a kind of 'universal affluence'.

Adam Smith did not believe that this could – or should – be done from the top down, by a species of constructivism, but by putting in place the proper conditions by which each family and each individual could choose the path of betterment within its own immediate world, on the reasonable grounds that this would be the most practical and intelligent way by which to proceed. (These are the very grounds of the famous 'principle of subsidiarity', about which so many in Europe these days speak so badly so much of the time.)

When Smith began his research, he was a professor of Christian moral philosophy, much influenced by the Jewish concern for 'orphans and widows', in short, the poor. As Meir Tamari makes plain in his magisterial study of Jewish economic thought down the ages, *With All Your Possessions*,[5] a compassionate concern for the poor is a pervasive Jewish theme, as it was not for Greeks, Romans, or most other peoples.

In all these ways, and others, Judaism has been a unique teacher of the human race. Those of us who are Christians must constantly be reminding ourselves how profound our debt to Judaism really is. In the history of liberty, political and economic, most of the things we take as first principles – even as common sense – we have derived from Judaism. Indeed, it is entirely proper for us to think of ourselves as being also children of Judah; from a Jewish point of view errant children, perhaps, but grateful descendants nonetheless.

---

[5] New York: The Free Press, 1987.

Afterword

Professor Jonathan Sacks

I AM DEEPLY GRATEFUL TO MICHAEL NOVAK, ROBERT DAVIDSON AND NORMAN BARRY for extending and enriching the argument I set out in my Hayek lecture. Michael Novak has re-articulated the Judaic vision with the grace and lucidity that makes him one of the towering moral commentators of our time. Norman Barry and Robert Davidson have each added lively caveats from perspectives slightly different from mine, the former arguing that the market is its own best moral guarantor, the latter reminding us of the variety and vitality of religious traditions and of their need constantly to be tested against reality. I particularly value Davidson's plea for our faith traditions to offer, in life as well as preaching, a compelling vision of hope.

All this is a way of thanking the Institute of Economic Affairs for its generosity in inviting a religious leader to engage in conversation with a distinguished gathering of economic thinkers. We need more conversations of this kind. Religious leaders have no privileged expertise on economics; nor do economists on matters theological. But our concerns overlap, and our perspectives differ, and it is the virtue of such encounters that they lead us beyond naïve economics on the one hand, simplistic theology on the other to a point where we can genuinely share our concerns for a more gracious social order.

Economists and theologians do have significant things to say to one another. Judaism, Christianity and Islam have each in their different ways wrestled with questions of wealth creation and distribution, relations between employers and employees, the tension between conserving and enhancing the environment, our duty to future generations and its implications for investment strategies, and so on. The great faith traditions invite us to think about such questions from the broadest of perspectives – the nature of human existence in a world only partially of our making – and they bring to the conversation large historical experience. At the same time they need constantly to be challenged and tested; never more so than now when the sheer pace of technological change heralds so many possibilities as well as threats to cherished certainties. If civilisation is conversation, or what the rabbis called 'argument for the sake of Heaven', then much depends on the quality of our listening and the diversity of voices that enter the debate. That is why I felt it was worthwhile to add a Judaic contribution without for a moment suggesting that it contains the final truth. In economics, there is no final truth.

Let me, then, re-state my case as simply as I can. Economists from Adam Smith onward have drawn our attention to the 'law of unintended consequences'. Not everything that happens in the social arena happens because the participants intended it. Results emerge that are different from anyone's conscious objective. That, as Albert O. Hirschman has so elegantly shown in his classic study, *The Passions and the Interests*, was one of the great early arguments for the capitalist system. The market, by harnessing self-interest, would produce results far transcending self-interest. Individual gain would lead to collective gain. Selfish motives would produce better results than selflessness.

The great gift of this startling paradox is that it came true. The market economy has indeed led to an astonishing revolution in living standards, educational opportunities, technological advance, health care, and all the other benefits that today make nostalgia for a golden past just that – nostalgia. Anyone who dreams of returning to the ordered grace of the 16th or 18th century might contemplate what it would be like to have a toothache then and now. We are collectively better off in a world in which the market harnesses our efforts to be individually better off.

It was Hayek's virtue to apply the law of unintended consequences not only to markets but also to political and social structures. It is precisely our inability accurately to foresee the results of particular policies that makes large-scale social engineering so disastrous. That is the 'fatal conceit'. Central planners get it wrong because nothing works out in the long run as we thought it would. Better the open texture of self-correcting mechanisms like the market. Hence Hayek, like Sir Karl Popper and Sir Isaiah Berlin, arrived at his rejection of central planning and the hyperactive state, and his vigorous defence of individual freedom. So far, so good.

But the market itself has unintended consequences, and these take time to appear. One of them is its sheer power, not only as a way of structuring transactions but as a way of dealing with other issues as well. The market becomes a metaphor, a paradigm, for much of human life. If products can be bought and sold, why not health or education or art or confidential information or reputations or relationships? Why not see marriage as a commercial contract for mutual advantage? Why not see children as commodities to be designed by genetic engineers and produced or terminated at will? Why not see all values as reducible to profit? Oscar Wilde defined the cynic as a person who knows the price of everything and the value of nothing. Is not the end product of the market the reign of universal cynicism?

Now this is standard anti-market rhetoric, and it is not my case to oppose the market. As I argued, the Judaic tradition holds the market and its attendant virtues in high regard. My case is different. It can be stated thus. *Ideas and institutions that have great benefit in their own domain have disastrous consequences when they are applied to another domain.*[1] Religion has great virtues in ordering communities. It has dire results when employed to govern states. Scientific method is supreme in explaining natural phenomena. It is catastrophic when used to prescribe human behaviour. Markets are the best way we know of structuring exchanges – goods to be bought and sold. They are far from the best way of ordering relationships or preserving goods whose value is not identical with their price.

This sounds self-evident. But self-evidence is no defence against error. The reason is this. Systems of thought are self-contained. They define a universe, but rarely do they signal the limits of that universe. There is no religious theory of the limits of religion. There is no scientific theory of the limits of science. To be sure, two major discoveries of the 20th century give us reason for humility. Godel's theorem establishes the limits of logic. Heisenberg's Uncertainty Principle suggests the limits of scientific

---

[1] Hayek himself devoted a whole book to this proposition. In *The Counter-Revolution of Science*, Indianapolis: Liberty Press, 1979, he distinguishes between science (the proper application of science to natural phenomena) and scientism (the improper application of science to human action).

observation. Both are ways within the system of postulating phenomena that lie beyond the system. But such humility is rare, and the opposite is more common.

The success of religion in the Middle Ages led it to expand beyond its proper borders and acquire not just influence but power. The success of science in the 17th and 18th centuries led thinkers to believe it contained answers to questions not just of natural causation but also of human purposes. Today the glittering paradigm is economics. Given the success of the market as against rival ways of matching supply and demand, why not reduce all relationships to transactions, all motives to self-interest, and all values to consumer choices? The short answer is – here as elsewhere – that what is valid in one domain is not necessarily true of another. From within the Judaic perspective (and surely within Christianity and Islam also) it is possible to see what a balanced social ecology might look like. Judaism values the free market. But it also values institutions that cannot be translated into market terms – the family, the Sabbath, a sense of possession as trusteeship, and so on. These do not compromise the integrity of the market, but they help shape the way its participants function as persons with serious moral commitments to values not reducible to the market. I think they make a difference.

I think they make a difference to how employers treat employees. I think they make a difference to how business people see their responsibilities to society, to local communities, to schools, to the impact of their decisions on individual lives. I think membership in certain groups – a religious community, for example – makes a difference to the salience of concepts like honour, trustworthiness, integrity and reputation. I think the presence or absence of strong family structures makes a difference to the time perspectives we bring to bear on decisions. I think that our religious traditions are one of the most powerful resources we have for teaching us that not everything we have an interest in doing should we do; for tempering desire with self-restraint; and for taking seriously the reality of other interests than our own. Unlike Norman Barry, I do not think that these virtues arise naturally from the market. They are essential to the health of the market, but they come from elsewhere.

I made these observations on the basis of my own limited

experience. I was therefore surprised to find them confirmed by a thinker whose expertise is quite different from my own. George Soros published *The Crisis of Global Capitalism* after I had delivered the lecture. I am in no position to evaluate his other contentions, but a central theme of the book precisely echoes the case I was making, in somewhat stronger language. He speaks of 'market fundamentalism' and of the 'transactional society' that emerges when 'the scope and influence of economic theory' expands 'beyond the confines that the postulates of an axiomatic system ought to impose'. The following paragraph gives a flavour of his approach:

'A transactional society undermines social values and loosens moral constraints. Social values express a concern for others. They imply that the individual belongs to a community, be it a family, a tribe, a nation, or humankind, whose interests must take precedence over the individual's self-interests. But a transactional market economy is anything but a community. Everybody must look out for his or her own interests and moral scruples can become an encumbrance in a dog-eat-dog world. In a purely transactional society, people who are not weighed down by any consideration for others can move around more easily and are likely to come out ahead . . . A purely transactional society could never exist, yet we are closer to it than at any time in history.'[2]

And perhaps in this context it is worth quoting another book, also published subsequently to the lecture, from a writer whose perspective is different from both Soros's and my own, Roger Scruton, who in his critique of modern culture writes:

'Faith exalts the human heart, by removing it from the market-place, making it sacred and unexchangeable. Under the jurisdiction of religion our deeper feelings are sacralised, so as to become raw material for the ethical life: the life lived in judgement. When faith declines, however, the sacred is unprotected from marauders; the heart can be captured and put on sale.'[3]

Is faith in decline? All I can say is that one of the institutions I

---

[2] George Soros, *The Crisis of Global Capitalism*, London: Little, Brown and Company, 1998, p.75.

[3] Roger Scruton, *An Intelligent Person's Guide to Modern Culture*, London: Duckworth, 1998, p.84.

am proudest of having had a share in creating is the Jewish Association of Business Ethics,[4] which regularly brings together leading business people and rabbinic experts in Jewish law to discuss practical dilemmas. It has proved hugely popular, and more than that. In extending its work to schools, it has shown sixth formers that business can and should be an ethical enterprise, and that an ancient tradition has compelling things to say in today's market-place.

Religion and economics are contrary voices, and we can only gain by dialogue between them. Religion will always urge us to look heavenward. Economists will remind us that we are creatures set on earth. Religion reminds us of our wider commitments. Economists insist that noble motives do not always yield the best results. There is no reason why both cannot accept the integrity of the other while checking its trespasses into domains not its own. That mutual testing of beliefs, candid, open, judged by the attentiveness of our listening as well as the cogency of our speech, is our best hope of not losing our way in the pace of our pursuits – and a fitting tribute to the memory of Friedrich Hayek who wrote: 'Paradoxical as it may appear, it is probably true that a successful free society will always in large measure be a tradition-bound society.'[5]

---

[4] Information on its work can be obtained from Lorraine Spector, Executive Director, The Jewish Association of Business Ethics, PO Box 3840, The Hyde, Colindale, London NW9 6LG.

[5] Friedrich Hayek, *The Constitution of Liberty*, London: Routledge, 1960, p.61.

THE IEA HAYEK
MEMORIAL LECTURES

1992   **Privatisation in Eastern Europe**
        Professor Jeffrey Sachs, Harvard University

1993   **Two Moral Ideals of Business**
        Professor Michael Novak, American Enterprise Institute,
        Washington DC

1994   **A New Framework for International
        Economic Relations**
        Dr Peter D. Sutherland, Director General,
        General Agreement on Tariffs and Trade

1995   **State and Society: Restoring the Balance**
        Rt Hon Francis Maude, Investment Banker and
        Chairman of the Government's De-regulation Task Force

1996   **New Zealand's Remarkable Reforms**
        Dr Donald T. Brash, Governor,
        Reserve Bank of New Zealand

1997   **The Transformation of Czech Society:
        Retrospect and Prospect**
        Vaclav Klaus, Prime Minister of the Czech Republic

1998   **Morals and Markets**
        Dr Jonathan Sacks, Chief Rabbi of the United Hebrew
        Congregations of the Commonwealth

Privatisation, Competition and Regulation

Stephen C. Littlechild

1. Austrian economists regard utilities as exceptional cases where regulation may be justified.

2. The long term aim for a public utility should be to '...turn as much as possible of that industry into a private, competitive and unregulated industry'. In the short term this may mean a 'considerable role for regulation'.

3. Price cap (RPI-X) regulation gives better efficiency incentives to companies than traditional US regulation and passes benefits on to consumers.

4. UK style privatisation and regulation put competition at the forefront whereas '...traditional US regulation for the most part suppressed it.'

5. In electricity, competition in generation has stimulated efficiency improvements but it is still not fully effective.

6. Big generators still set wholesale prices most of the time and the government's 'stricter consents' policy for gas-fired plant hinders entry to generation: that policy is the 'most significant obstacle to a more competitive market'.

7. Competition to supply industrial consumers has resulted in large numbers of companies switching to new suppliers and prices have fallen considerably.

8. Introducing competition to supply domestic consumers was a major logistical exercise. The cost was more than justified by the lower prices and other benefits now flowing from competition.

9. Some of the changes to utility regulation now proposed by the government will not be helpful - such as the qualification to the regulators' duty to promote competition.

10. The next step should be a further transfer, from government to consumers, of control over the utilities. A challenge is to find ways by which competition can substitute for regulation in remaining monopoly sectors.

The Institute of Economic Affairs

2 Lord North Street, Westminster, London SW1P 3LB
Telephone: 0171 799 3745 Facsimile: 0171 799 2137
E-mail: iea@iea.org.uk Internet: http://www.iea.org.uk   ISBN 0-255 36480-6

£5.00

Hayek, Currency Competition and European Monetary Union

Otmar Issing
With Commentaries by
Lawrence H. White
Roland Vaubel

In the 1999 IEA Hayek Memorial Lecture, reprinted in Occasional Paper 111, Otmar Issing, the eminent monetary economist and one of Europe's most influential central bankers, discusses currency competition and European Monetary Union.

Professor Issing argues that choosing a '...Hayekian discovery process as a route to monetary union' would have been too risky. However, the introduction of the euro has triggered '...a kind of Hayekian discovery process' which gives more scope for the private sector to '...enhance the quality of the medium-of-exchange and store-of-value functions of money.'

This Occasional Paper also includes commentaries by two other distinguished economists - Professors Lawrence H.White and Roland Vaubel - who criticise Professor Issing's views. There is then an Afterword by Issing.

The Institute of Economic Affairs
2 Lord North Street, Westminster, London SW1P 3LB
Telephone: 0171 799 3745 Facsimile: 0171 799 2137
E-mail: iea@iea.org.uk Internet: http://www.iea.org.uk   ISBN 0-255 36481-4

£6.00